XB York, M. J.
WIL Woodrow Wilson

4/2017

Woodrow Wilson

BY M. J. YORK

Published by The Child's World®
1980 Lookout Drive • Mankato, MN 56003-1705
800-599-READ • www.childsworld.com

Photographs ©: North Wind Picture Archives, cover, 1; Picture History/Newscom, 4, 11; Everett Historical/Shutterstock Images, 7; Ken Welsh/Newscom, 8; Everett Collection/Newscom, 12; World History Archive/Newscom, 15; AP Images, 17, 21; akg-images/Newscom, 18

Copyright © 2017 by The Child's World®
All rights reserved. No part of this book may be reproduced or utilized in any form or by any means without written permission from the publisher.

ISBN 9781503816503
LCCN 2016945647

Printed in the United States of America
PA02322

ABOUT THE AUTHOR

M. J. York is a children's book editor and author. She loves writing and learning about history. She lives with her family in Minnesota.

Table of Contents

CHAPTER ONE
Declaring War.................. 5

CHAPTER TWO
Witness to War 9

CHAPTER THREE
Professor and President Wilson.........13

CHAPTER FOUR
World at War 19

Timeline 22

Glossary 23

To Learn More............ 24

Index 24

Woodrow Wilson was known for his passion for peace.

CHAPTER ONE

Declaring War

It was April 2, 1917. President Woodrow Wilson had to give a speech. World War I was raging in Europe. The United States was at peace. Wilson wanted the country to stay that way. But the war was changing. Wilson had to make a decision.

The war had started three years ago. It was dividing countries in Europe. France and the United Kingdom were on one side. Germany and Austria-Hungary were on the other. German submarines attacked enemy ships. Many people died.

Germany sank several U.S. ships in early 1917. This made many Americans angry.

Then British spies found a secret note. Germany wanted Mexico to fight against the United States. The note made many Americans even angrier.

Wilson was tired. He had not slept the night before. He did not want to go to war. But he felt Germany left him no option. Wilson went to the U.S. **Congress**. The president cannot **declare** war by himself. Only Congress can.

Wilson stood before Congress. The room was full of people. He spoke about the war. He said German attacks were a war against everyone. Wilson asked Congress to declare war against Germany. He wanted the world to be "safe for **democracy**."

Wilson addressing Congress on April 2, 1917

Wilson was known for his speeches. His speech convinced Congress. The country entered the war four days later. Wilson wanted to stay at peace. But now he wanted to win the war. After the war, he would help make peace again.

The Civil War impacted Wilson for the rest of his life.

CHAPTER TWO

Witness to War

Thomas Woodrow Wilson was born on December 28, 1856. His family lived in Staunton, Virginia. He had two sisters and one brother. Everyone called him Tommy. His family moved to Georgia. In 1861 the U.S. Civil War began. Tommy's father was a minister. He also worked for the army. Tommy's mother was a nurse. One of Tommy's earliest memories was seeing wounded soldiers. His mother nursed them back to health. He would never forget how terrible war was.

Education was important to the Wilsons. But Tommy faced challenges. He had poor eyesight. He also might have had **dyslexia**. Tommy could not read until he was 10. But his father taught him religion at home. He taught Tommy history, too. Tommy also liked to play baseball.

At age 16, Tommy went away to school. He studied many subjects. He learned how to write and give speeches.

Tommy went to college two years later. He went to Princeton University in New Jersey. He made many friends there. He liked to **debate**. Tommy graduated in 1879. Then he went to law school. Tommy became a lawyer. He worked briefly in Atlanta, Georgia. But he was bored and lonely. He had few friends. And he wanted romance.

Wilson studied political science and history in college.

Wilson with his wife, Ellen, and his three daughters, Jessie, Eleanor, and Margaret

CHAPTER THREE

Professor and President Wilson

In 1883, Wilson met a woman in church. Her name was Ellen Axson. It was love at first sight. They went on picnics. They talked about books. They got married on June 24, 1885. By 1889 they had three daughters.

Wilson went back to school during this time. He no longer wanted to be a lawyer. He wanted to be a professor instead. He studied history and government.

He finished school. He also taught at two colleges. Then Princeton University offered him a job. It was his dream to return to Princeton. So the family moved to New Jersey in 1890. He was a popular teacher. People came to hear his speeches and lessons. He wrote books and many articles.

In 1902 Princeton needed a new president. The university board picked Wilson. Wilson changed how classes were taught. He had new buildings built. He gave speeches around the country. Wilson was becoming famous.

The **Democratic Party** liked Wilson. New Jersey party leaders wanted him to lead the state. They wanted him to be governor. They picked him to run in September 1910. That fall he gave many speeches. He won over the hearts of voters. Wilson was elected governor on November 8.

Wilson was the 13th president of Princeton University.

Wilson found out leaders in New Jersey were dishonest. Government officials took money to do favors. They were paid to pass laws for people. Wilson promised to stop this. He passed laws to change the state government. Democratic leaders noticed him. They wanted him to run for president.

Three people ran for president in 1912. Wilson ran as the Democrat. William Howard Taft ran as the Republican. He was the current president. Theodore Roosevelt ran as a third party. Wilson won. He took office on March 4, 1913.

As president, Wilson worked on important issues. He changed tax laws. He made new rules for businesses. Wilson gave speeches to explain his ideas. He was the first president to hold press conferences. Journalists could ask him questions at the conferences.

Wilson was the first U.S. president who had served as president of a university.

He spoke in front of Congress, too. Earlier presidents did not make speeches there. Wilson's term was going well. But soon everything would change.

The British ship *Lusitania* was sunk by a German submarine torpedo. More than 120 Americans died.

CHAPTER FOUR

World at War

On July 28, 1914, war broke out. Austria-Hungary declared war on Serbia. Soon most countries in Europe were fighting. World War I had started. Wilson's wife Ellen fell ill. She died on August 6, 1914. Wilson was sad. But he had to continue leading the country.

The United States did not take a side in the war. But it traded with Great Britain and France. The United States was also friends with Serbia. It was less friendly with Germany and Austria-Hungary. In May 1915, Germans sunk a British ship.

Americans were on board. They died. The United States still did not enter the war.

Wilson ran for a second term in 1916. The election was close. He won.

At this time, the United States faced many **social** problems. Women wanted the right to vote. African Americans wanted more rights. Wilson did little to help. He was against women voting. Later, he supported it. Women got the right to vote in 1920.

Peace ended after Wilson's speech to Congress. The U.S. military was small. It had to grow quickly. A **draft** forced men to fight. American troops helped win World War I. Fighting ended on November 11, 1918.

World leaders had to make a peace **treaty**. Wilson helped. He wanted to prevent other wars. He had 14 main ideas for peace. He wrote them down.

Wilson (far right) worked with the leaders of Italy, Great Britain, and France to create a peace treaty in 1919.

They were called the "Fourteen Points." The leaders used some of his ideas. But the U.S. Congress did not sign the agreement.

In October 1919, Wilson had a **stroke**. Wilson left office in March 1921. It was the end of his presidency. The United States never signed the peace agreement. Wilson's health did not get better. He died on February 3, 1924. He was 67 years old.

Wilson made many changes during his presidency. He started new practices, such as press conferences. He led the country through World War I. He worked hard to keep world peace.

TIMELINE

1850

← **December 28, 1856** Thomas Woodrow Wilson is born in Staunton, Virginia.

← **1879** Wilson graduates from Princeton University.

← **June 24, 1885** Wilson marries Ellen Axson.

← **1890** Wilson becomes a professor at Princeton.

← **1902** Wilson becomes the president of Princeton.

← **November 8, 1910** Wilson is elected governor of New Jersey.

← **March 4, 1913** Wilson takes office as the 28th president of the United States.

← **July 28, 1914** Austria-Hungary declares war on Serbia and World War I begins.

← **August 6, 1914** Wilson's wife Ellen dies.

← **November 8, 1916** Wilson is reelected president.

← **April 2, 1917** Wilson calls for the country to enter World War I.

← **October 1919** Wilson suffers a stroke.

← **February 3, 1924** Wilson dies at age 67.

1930

GLOSSARY

Congress (KONG-gris) Congress is the branch of the U.S. government that makes laws. Wilson spoke to Congress.

debate (di-BATE) To debate is to discuss different opinions. Wilson liked to debate.

declare (di-CLARE) To declare is to announce something formally. The president cannot declare war on his or her own.

democracy (dih-MOK-ruh-see) A democracy is a type of government that is decided by people voting. Wilson wanted to protect democracy during World War I.

Democratic Party (dem-uh-KRAT-ik PAHR-tee) The Democratic Party is a political party in the United States. Wilson was a member of the Democratic Party.

draft (DRAFT) A draft is a law that makes people join the military. The government held a draft during World War I.

dyslexia (dis-LEK-see-uh) Dyslexia is a condition of the brain that makes it difficult to read. Wilson might have had dyslexia.

social (SOH-shul) Something that is social has to do with the way people live together. Wilson faced big social issues as president.

stroke (STROK) A stroke is a medical problem caused when oxygen cannot reach the brain. Wilson suffered a stroke.

treaty (TREE-tee) A treaty is a formal agreement. Wilson worked with world leaders on a peace treaty after World War I.

TO LEARN MORE

In the Library

Adamson, Thomas K. *World War I.* Mankato, MN: The Child's World, 2015.

Brassey, Richard. *The Story of World War I.* London, UK: Orion Publishing Group, 2014.

Frith, Margaret. *Who Was Woodrow Wilson?* New York: Grosset & Dunlap, 2015.

On the Web

Visit our Web site for links about Woodrow Wilson: **childsworld.com/links**

Note to Parents, Teachers, and Librarians: We routinely verify our Web links to make sure they are safe and active sites. So encourage your readers to check them out!

INDEX

American Civil War, 9
Axson, Ellen, 13, 19

Congress, 6–7, 17, 20, 21

Democrat, 16

Germany, 5–6, 19
governor, 14

New Jersey, 10, 14, 16

peace, 5, 7, 20, 21
Princeton University, 10, 14

Roosevelt, Theodore, 16

speech, 5, 7, 10, 14, 16, 17, 20

Taft, William Howard, 16

World War I, 5, 19, 20, 21